E.M. Sol is an emerging young writer consistently writing for the past three to five years through school works and busy days, whether those be poems, short stories, or novels. This is his first book to be published. E.M. Sol has a deep and great passion for writing and is hoping to share his works with the world and become an inspiration for other writers.

To Mika, the biggest inspiration for me going forward with my
life, and someone who I hold dearly in my heart.
To you, my dearest sister.

E.M. Sol

Museum of Reflections

Austin Macauley Publishers™

London • Cambridge • New York • Sharjah

ISBN – 9789948762157 – (Paperback)
ISBN – 9789948762164 – (E-Book)

Application Number: MC-10-01-6050042
Age Classification: E

Printer Name: iPrint Global Ltd
Printer Address: Witchford, England

First Published 2024
AUSTIN MACAULEY PUBLISHERS FZE
Sharjah Publishing City
P.O Box [519201]
Sharjah, UAE
www.austinmacauley.ae
+971 655 95 202

Table of Contents

Moonless Nights

Every night, I ask the stars of how you're doing
of how you're doing up there,
I miss you more than ever, and it seems the moon silently agrees.

Moonless nights, I miss your presence,
and perhaps, on the break of a new dawn,
we can renew ourselves for the day.

Entranced

A moonlight serenade;
a moonlit embrace.

I am entranced by your beauty, and your glamor.

Perhaps it wasn't your looks I fell for,
but you.

I had fallen for you,
and with each hallway my heart would find itself in
they'd always lead back to you.

Admiration of the Moon

There are nights
where I lose track of time
admiring the moon

For when I see the moon,
I think of her.

I think,

of how she bathes
under the warmth
of the moon's light,

of how the moonlight
let's go of your sweet embrace
the moment the sun comes up.

Moonlight through the Window

She was the moonlight
hidden behind the curtains;
the moonlight that awaited me
as I stepped outside of my doorstep.

The Moon's Thoughts

Oh, how the moon sighs
when you're not around
and oh, how I wish to tell you
that whenever the sun renews itself for another day's work,

it always thinks of you.

Stars

Stars in the night sky
could never hold a candle
to the incandescent flowers
that cradle me in their warm embrace,

the flowers that blossom in your heart…
entrancing me ever so lightly.

Constellations

You will always be

my favorite star;
my favorite constellation,

that lights up the night skies.

Reflecting

You, as a whole

will always shine as bright
as the moon reflecting the sun's light,

will always radiate the warmth
that the sun gives off
under the veiled blue tinted skies.

Letters

If you open the letters I've left you
under your moonlit doorstep.

Look to the stars, and I'll be there.

Whether it be day or night,
dusk or dawn.

I'll be the star that stays;
the star that sings an incandescent ode
for your sleepless nights.

Fascination with the Moon

I've always admired the moon

and how it chases after the sun, endlessly.

I wonder, how does it not get tired?

Tired of chasing after something just barely out of reach.

Love of the Moon

I love the moon
not for its beauty and elegance,

but because it stays the same…
how it never leaves me.

Dawn

Whether or not the moon
will depart soon
I can't tell.

The dawn calls to me
as does the rising of the sun

If only the moon could stay forever
and not disappear every so often
then perhaps I could enjoy
this moonlit view of mine.

Elegant Luna

Oh, elegant moon
for why do you weep?

The sun may set
however temporary it may be
it always comes back, doesn't it?

Cry no further,
my beautiful moon
for I will never leave you.

Leave your sorrows behind
for unlike the sun,

my warmth will extend
even to the coldest reaches.

Comes and Goes

Why must you leave me,
my lovely moon?

Replacing me once again
for the sun

that merely comes and goes
when I can stay,
for as long as you wish.

Grasping at Nothing

I still believe in this delusion of mine
that I can reach the moon,
and hold it tight, in a warm embrace.

But it's getting tiring
chasing after something
that's just barely out of reach

I can see it with my eyes
how lovely you are,
and how lonely the incandescent moonlight
that you emit

covers me every night.

Oh, I wish that you'd come to me,
the moon that sits still every midnight
and I can only admire
the melody it plays whenever it sees the sun.

Morning Dew

To the sun I sang
of the ocean song
and the morning dew.

To the moon, I swore
of the blooming nights
and the evening's calm.

Sun and Moon

For he was like the sun;
shining golden for her,
radiating the warmth of home.

And I, was the moon.

Merely reflecting the light that had passed,
radiating the calmness of the night.

Where Did You Go?

People often talk of the moonlight
but never of where it came from.

People often talk
of how happy I am all the time…

but never of where it came from,
of who it comes from.

Fragments

In the end, we are all fragments
pieces of moonlight echoing through an empty room
of the people who were once in our lives.

People who meant something to us, once.

However, they are now gone
and we are left to ponder,

the pieces of their soul that they once shared
the pieces that built us up through the years,

is it right for us to let go of that?

Is it right for us to let go of a past that never fades,
a past that never lingers nor disappears,
the frightening past that we so often look back to.

Why Did You Leave?

I wish the moon wouldn't leave me
whenever the sun rises

because whenever it does,
so does the moonlight that I bask in

because whenever it does,
I have to wait
until it comes back to me,

once more.

You Always Come Back

Words can never come back
but how come,
the ones you left for me

always find a way back

to each crevice of my heart
like how the moon comes back
as soon as the sun sets.

Conversations with the Moon

Each time the moon passed by
under my balcony, in the dead of night
it would assure me
that you were sleeping safe and sound.

I had told the moon,
that suddenly, all the songs were about you;
every star in the night sky
painted a picture of you.

Reflections

Who are we, if not reflections of our past?

Oh, my little dove

for why do you stare at the moon so blankly?

Do you see the reflection of yourself within it,

and do you see how wonderful it is?

Us

Our love was like a fleeting dream

which is why

I find it hard to fall asleep nowadays

as I am reminded of our past thoughts of us.

Skies

It's not fair whenever you go out
and speak of how beautiful the skies are

but then take one glance at a mirror
and find yourself utterly disappointed

when the heavens put in the same efforts
into making both of you.

She Was the Only One

"Do you really love me," she asks.

Little does she know,

I have no more words left for others

because I've exhausted all of them by the mere thought of her.

How Do You Love?

Everyone has their own ways of loving.

Some choose to give their warmth to others,
some, spend their dear time with those they love.

But all in all
everyone's unique way of loving
is what makes us all special.

How do I love, you ask?

I would pick up the fallen stars, and drop them by your
windowsill
so that when you awake
the first thing you'll see are the stars;

I would hold the sun still
if it meant your radiance would shine
even brighter.

Solace in Another

Sometimes the solace we find in isolation
isn't what we need

but rather

the warmth of another person's presence.

Tomorrow's Worries

For do we have the right
to wish for tomorrow to come
when we haven't even experienced
the light reflected upon during the night
and the warmth of a new dawn?

What Ifs

Oh, my love

if only tomorrow had come for us sooner

perhaps we'd have had

one more day to cherish

in each other's arms.

Incandescence

I profess my love to you

with an incandescent ode;

one to light up the night sky

with stars as bright as you.

Her

Her hands were warm
but her eyes were cold

the softness of her touch
enveloping the edges of my soul

her starlit gaze
etched into the back of my mind

reflections of what used to be
of what could've been

stuck on my mind
like the echoes of your voice
telling me to let go.

Is There Anything Left to Come Back To?

It's already winter.

We can't just keep coming back
when there's really nothing to come back to

looking at my reflection in the mirror,
do I still wish that you were next to me?

I'm getting tired of waiting
for you to make a move

because by the time you've made one
the warmth I have in my heart for you
is already long gone.

Shelled Heart

This old, worn-out heart of mine
barely beating still.

I locked it away; away from harm's way,
away to keep the pain at bay.

This old, rusting heart of mine

barely beating still.

You Were the Spring

If flowers only bloom during spring,

how come the ones in my heart blossom whenever you're around me?

If the winter is as cold as they say it is,

how is it that I still feel your warmth around my heart?

As days go by in a flash,

my first and last thought will always be

of you.

And You Still Are

In the peak of the spring season

the Sakura leaves blossom.

Whenever I feel lost,

one look into your eyes helps me find my way;

as if they shine, illuminating my way forward

to where I'm supposed to be…

by your side.

Shining

Your eyes shine
like the water
reflecting the calm moon.
I envy the summer nights
for they get to hold you
in its warm embrace
under the moonlight.

Comfort in a Person

Your presence radiates comfort
within the confined spaces of my mending heart.

Love, if only you knew of all the conversations I have
with the moon, and with the stars.

The moon – it softly speaks to me
of all your wonders and how you shine just as bright as it does.

The stars – they sing to me a sweet melody
of how stars form whenever you smile.

These little conversations I have with them,
I tell them of how I love to share little fragments of myself
to you.

I'm not in love, but I'm definitely falling for you, dear.

Stargazing

I ask the moon to shower you with stars,

knowing it gets to watch over you as you rest.

In the morning, I pray to the sun

to cover you in its warmth

in times where I'm not by your side.

Fantasies

You were just a fantasy;

something I'd want to relive

and I'll just be a fleeting dream;

you won't even remember me.

Why I Write

I write

about the seasons, about the stars

about the flowers, and about the nature

because they're a constant…

Unlike people,

they don't change.

In the Absence of You

It feels like I was holding onto something

that was never there,

gripping so tightly at your hand

I didn't want to – I don't want to

don't want to let go.

Little Miss Delightful

Maybe it was the way she smiled

or perhaps the way she looked at me when we were alone.

I don't know why, I'm not sure how, but
it seems I've fallen for her

more than I expected to.

Only with You

I've never been in love

the way I am with you.

Your presence alone

is enough to keep me warm

underneath the mistletoe.

I Miss You

Every night
I wish to slow the clammy hands of time.

Every day
I want to just live in those same moments

together with you.

A New Dawn

In the break of a new day, of a new dawn

the first thought I have is of you

and at the end of the night, of the moonfall

my prayers include you, and of your happiness and safety.

Dreaming

You're the only dream I seek.

With every glance I steal,

I fall deeper and deeper for you,

leaving me utterly entranced.

I Long for You

Maybe it wasn't a matter of me
missing your presence, or the memories we shared

but rather,

it was just that I missed you.

Reminiscing

I reminisce of the serene seasons
but I find no joy in them anymore.

I look at the moon and the stars with a sorrowful gaze
because I no longer find the same happiness
I once found in them.

Now,

I look at this field of purple roses
and think to myself
of how much I've fallen for you
and how happy I am by your side.

Flowers

Flowers may wither away

but my love will always be here to stay

my heart is a garden filled with flowers

these flowers

made into a bouquet

all for you.

Lights That Guide Me

The lights in the night sky

illuminate my way forward

they all lead me to you.

Bouquets in Your Arms

I have a fascination with flowers

and how the little details represent so much

when looking at a field of flowers, it makes me wonder

how beautiful they'd look in a bouquet

or even better

how lovely that bouquet would be in your arms.

Winter

The winter has passed,

yet I can still feel your warmth

the spring is here,

but I still miss your presence

summer and autumn is rolling around the corner

and yet

I can't find the right words to say to you.

Taken Aback

I have no more words left for others;

no poems left to write, and no songs left to sing,

for you have taken them all, just as you have taken my heart.

It's Always Been You

The stars,

every night they speak to me of your wonders

they tell me of how your eyes shine

where the stars don't

and that your smile

radiates comfort wherever you go.

Don't Settle for Less

The sun doesn't wait for the moon to catch up

so why should you wait for something that won't work?

A Star Yet Seen, A Serenade Yet Sung

A moonlit serenade

your heart set ablaze, encompassing my gentle soul

the kindles of our souls touch, and for a moment

both our hands and hearts entwine

for a moment
the moon and the sun had come to a halt,

they had stopped and stole glances at each other.

I Want to Be Yours

I don't want to just be an option

I want to be the answer

maybe you were the right person

but it was just the wrong time

maybe

maybe you were the one for me

in another lifetime.

Conversations with the Stars

If the sun could speak,

it'd talk of the countless times you've made my days better
just by being there.

If the moon could sing,

it'd sing a sweet melody of how your beautiful smile
lights up my darkest nights.

Comparisons

The stars, they may shine

but they could never shine the way your eyes do

the sun, it may be bright

but it could never be as bright as your smile

and the moon, its beauty is amazing as it is divine;

but, the moon – it could never, ever compare to you.

Guardian Angels

Knowing that the moon and the stars
watch over you during times when I'm not there,

knowing that the sun
watches over you during the mornings when I'm not around

reassures me that you're in safe hands,
and that the stars, the moon, and the sun

guide you, and protect you.

I Was Never Hers to Begin With

He was everything
she had ever hoped for in a boy;

tall and handsome,
fair and brave,
smart and talented…
he was everything I wasn't.

For I was merely a poet
one who'd utter verses
that spoke of the moon
as if I'd ever come close
to ever touching it.

Passage of Time

Sometimes,
people come into our lives
just as fast as they leave.

A lot of these times,
these people were the right person for us
but it was just the wrong time.

Don't look for love
just to satisfy your loneliness
love is give and take;
you receive just as much love as you give out.

So, in time for spring rolling right around the corner
I hope that you find
a sweet spring breeze
to fill your heart with warmth
just as it did with mine.

A Change of Pace

Of the wind,
and of an ocean song

in this sea of gray bricks
you are the patch of green that colors my soul, the small, special
assortment of flowers in a field of grass

you're the warmth I feel through the breeze
during the long summer days

and you are the breeze
that I'd let in time and time again
to feel the warmth of the spring.

Museums

We are all museums

filled with the memories

and the habits we pick up

from those we once loved.